The United States soccer team listens to the Star Spangled Banner before the start of the 2011 CONCACAF Gold Cup match against Mexico at the Rose Bowl on June 25, 2011, in Pasadena, California.

U.S. MEN'S TEAM

NEW STARS ON THE FIELD

Abbeville Press Publishers

New York · London

A portion of the book's proceeds are donated to
the **Hugo Bustamante AYSO Playership Fund,**
a national scholarship program to help ensure
that no child misses the chance to play AYSO
Soccer. Donations to the fund cover the cost
of registration and a uniform for a child in need.

Text by Illugi Jökulsson

For the original edition
Design and layout: Ólafur Gunnar Guðlaugsson

For the English-language edition
Editor: Joan Strasbaugh
Production manager: Louise Kurtz
Designer: Ada Rodriguez
Copy editor: Ken Samuelson

PHOTOGRAPHY CREDITS

Getty Images
2, 6, 12, 14, 16, 19, 21, 23, 25, 26, 27, 28, 29, 31, 32, 33, 34, 36, 39, 40, 41, 43, 44, 46, 48, 49, 51, 52, 53, 55, 57,
58, 59, 60, 61

Shutterstock
9, 42, 57 (Beckham), 63

All statistics current through the 2012–2013 season unless otherwise noted

First published in the United States of America in 2014 by Abbeville Press, 137 Varick Street,
New York, NY 10013

First edition
10 9 8 7 6 5 4 3 2 1

Library of Congress Cataloging-in-Publication Data

Illugi Jvkulsson.
  U.S.A. men's team : stars on the field / by Illugi Jvkulsson.
    pages cm. — (World soccer legends)
  Summary: "Tells the story of U.S. Men's National Team from the formation of the U.S. Football Association
100 years ago to its six consecutive trips to the World Cup"— Provided by publisher.
  Includes bibliographical references and index.
  ISBN 978-0-7892-1180-4 (hardback) — ISBN 0-7892-1180-7 (hardcover) 1. Soccer—United States—History—
Juvenile literature. 2. Soccer teams—United States—History—Juvenile literature. 3. World Cup (Soccer)—
Juvenile literature. I. Title.
  GV944.U5I55 2014
  796.334—dc23
                    2013046920

For bulk and premium sales and for text adoption procedures, write to Customer Service Manager,
Abbeville Press, 137 Varick Street, New York, NY 10013, or call 1-800-ARTBOOK.

Visit Abbeville Press online at **www.abbeville.com.**

CONTENTS

THE FIRST KICKS

Native Mesoamericans probably played the first real ball games in the Americas. They developed undeniably brutal games played with large rubber balls as early as 1500 BC. When settlers from England arrived in Massachusetts in the early 17th century they discovered the native Algonquian tribes playing a game called pasuckuakohowog, which translates to "a gathering to play ball with the foot." This game seems to have died out as the natives were pushed inland by the new arrivals.

The Europeans brought with them different ball games, mostly variations on large scale types of football. In England, the first football rules were drawn up at Cambridge University in 1848 and then in 1863 the English Football Association was founded. It standardized the various rules then in use and this date marks the formal beginning of "association football."

Soon, both the early "associaton football" and the English *rugby* were being played in the U.S. Rugby was evolving into what has since been called *American football* and therefore "association football" was abbreviated as "soccer." The term orginated in England but came to be used mainly in the U.S. and Canada.

PASUCKUAKOHOWOG was played on large beaches or wide open spaces. The two goals were half a mile wide and up to one mile apart. The sizes of the competing teams varied, 500 players was common and there are reports of up to 1,000. The game was quite violent and players often had to quit with broken bones or other serious injuries. They wore war paint and even disguised themselves to avoid retaliation after the games, which could last for hours and even into the next day.

It has to be said that at the time football and similar ball games in Europe were no less violent, and sometimes even more so. But after each game of pasuckuakohowog the two teams sat down with the spectators for a large celebratory feast. Now, that would be something after exciting World Cup soccer games!

Native Americans playing pasuckuakohowog. Imagine that kind of a crowd on a modern soccer field!

A soccer ball from the early 20th century. It was made of leather with a rubber balloon inside. When it rained it could become quite heavy. Then it could be rather risky business to head the ball powerfully!

THE AMERICAN FOOTBALL ASSOCIATION

was founded in 1884. It was the first attempt to form an organizing body for soccer. The AFA established the American Cup and organized various other league and cup competitions. It was replaced by the United States Football Association, which was recognized by FIFA in 1913 as the official governing body of soccer in the U.S.

FOOTBALL BECOMES SOCCER

The U.S. Football Association became the U.S. Soccer Football Association in 1945. Then in 1974 the both "football" and "association" were dropped, resulting in the United States Soccer Federation.

A STRONG START

D·W·GRIFFITH'S
COLOSSAL SPECTACLE

1916

INTOLERANCE
· A SUN PLAY OF THE AGES ·
THE BIRTH OF A NATION

In the summer of 1916 World War I ravaged Europe. The U.S. was not yet a participant and neither were the Scandinavian countries of Sweden and Norway. Their soccer federations invited a national team from the new U.S. federation to play a few games. In early August the U.S. team crossed the Atlantic, where German U-boats were on the prowl, and fortunately the team's ship was not attacked.

On August 16 the U.S. team played its very first game, drawing a heated 1–1 game against an all-star team from Sweden's capital Stockholm. John "Rabbit" Heminsley scored the first goal in a U.S. national jersey before 20,000 mostly Swedish fans.

Then on August 21 the first official international game of the U.S. was played against a full Swedish national team in Stockholm. About 21,000 were in the crowd, including the King of Sweden, Gustav V. Even though the Swedish team had vastly more experience, the U.S. opened the scoring. Sources do not agree as to who scored the first offical goal for the U.S. Either it was defender Dick Spalding of Pennsylvania or the captain himself, Thomas Swords of Massachusetts with a fine individual effort. Either way, two additional goals were scored by Charles Ellis of New York and Harry Cooper of New Jersey after a fantastic run down the left. The Swedes could only respond with two goals of their own, so the U.S. had won their first official international match.

On September 3 the U.S. team then played Norway in Kristiania (later Oslo) and drew 1–1 in spite of losing two players to injury during the game. No substitutes were allowed at that point. Ellis scored again.

In addition to these games, the U.S. team played three more unofficial games during this trip, winning two and losing one.

THE NEXT GAMES

After World War I ended in 1918, U.S. players again traveled to Scandinavia in 1919 and 1920 but not as an official national team. The next official games were played in 1924 at the summer Olympics in Paris. In the first round of the soccer competition the U.S. defeated Estonia by a single penalty converted by Andy Straden (born in Scotland) and then lost badly to a very strong Uruguayan team. After the Olympics, the U.S. played two friendlies, defeating Poland but then losing to Ireland.

The team that toured Scandinavia, with officials and substitute players that didn't take part in the games. In the back row, from left: Ellis, Tintle, Spalding, Cahill (secretary of the USFA), Burgin, Smith (coach). In the middle row: Robertson, Murray, Clarke, Blakey. In the front row: Ford, Swords, Heminsley, Diedrichsen, Cooper.

THE LINEUP OF THE FIRST INTERNATIONAL GAME OF THE U.S.:

THOMAS MURRAY   THOMAS SWORDS

JAMES ROBERTSON   "RABBIT" HEMINSLEY

GEORGE TINTLE   NEIL CLARKE   MATT DIEDRICHSEN

DICK SPALDING   HARRY COOPER

CHARLES ELLIS

JAMES FORD

The US goalkeeper Jimmy Douglas has just snatched the ball from famed Argentinian striker Guillermo Stábile (sitting down) during the semifinal game between the U.S. and Argentina. On the left U.S. attacker Bart McGhee is helping in defense. Argentina won 6–1, but the U.S. had started the competition admirably.

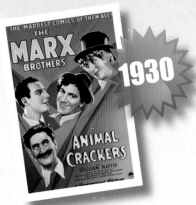

THIRD PLACE AT THE FIRST WORLD CUP!

WORLD CUP 1930
Uruguay

Date	Opponent	Result	U.S. Goals
7-13-30	Belgium	3–0 ○	McGhee, Florie, Patenaude
7-17-30	Paraguay	3–0 ○	Patenaude 3
7-26-30	Argentina	1–6 ○	Brown

The first World Cup was held in Montevideo, Uruguay in the summer of 1930. All members of FIFA, the International Football Association, were invited but few teams from Europe showed up. The journey took two months by ship and in the middle of the Great Depression many players simply could not afford to make the trip. The U.S. team did however decide to go.

The team had not played any games since 1928, when it was humiliated by Argentina in the first round of the Summer Olympics in Amsterdam, losing 11–2. Other sports in the U.S. had grown much faster than soccer in the previous decade, so few people expected much from the U.S. at World Cup. But the team did better than anybody had even hoped, winning its preliminary group ahead of Belgium

THE SAME TEAM PLAYED ALL THREE GAMES AT THE 1930 WORLD CUP:

JIMMY GALLAGHER JAMES BROWN

ALEXANDER WOOD BILLY GONSALVES

JIMMY DOUGLAS

RAPHAEL TRACEY

BERT PATENAUDE

GEORGE MOORHOUSE TOM FLORIE

ANDY AULD BART MCGHEE

THE WINNER IS ...

URUGUAY

Overcame neighbors Argentina 4–2 in the final.

and Paraguay. Bart McGhee scored the USA's first World Cup goal in the 23rd minute against Belgium, hitting the ball perfectly as it rebounded off the crossbar after a Gonsalves shot.

Four days later, Bert Patenaude of Massachusetts scored the first hat trick in the history of the World Cup against Paraguay. There was some confusion as to who scored the U.S.'s second goal, Patenaude or captain Florie, but FIFA later ruled in favor of Patenaude.

With these two fine victories the U.S. topped its group and was rewarded with a place in the semifinals against mighty Argentina. The game was even until U.S. midfielder Tracey suffered a serious knee injury about 10–20 minutes into the game. As no substitutes were allowed he tried to play on, but had to withdraw at half time. The U.S. then played one man short. It didn't help either that goalkeeper Jimmy Douglas also injured himself and

could only limp for most of the second half. All things considered the result was not that bad, especially after a late consolation goal scored by outside left James Brown.

No special game for the bronze medal was held at this World Cup but FIFA listed the U.S. as finishing in third place. This is still the team's highest World Cup place, and through 2010 the only time a team from outside Europe or South America has finished in the top three.

Back row from left: Millar (coach), Gallagher, Wood, Douglas, Moorhouse, Tracey, Auld. Front row from left: Brown, Gonsalves, Patenaude, Florie, McGhee.

NO LUCK IN ITALY

1934

THE WINNER IS ...

ITALY

Defeated Czechoslovakia 2–1 in the hard fought final.

Four years later the U.S. couldn't repeat its success at the 1934 World Cup in Italy. The U.S. qualified by beating Mexico 4–2 in the two teams' first (but definitely not last!) encounter, with Aldo Donelli of Pennsylvania scoring all four goals. This was the first time an American scored four goals in a national game, a feat that Landon Donovan would repeat in the 2003 Gold Cup. At the World Cup itself the U.S. was easily eliminated in the first round by the very strong home team, which did end up World Champions.

Aldo Donelli

WORLD CUP 1934
Italy

Date	Opponent	Result	U.S. Goal
5-27-34	Italy	1–7 ○	Donelli

15

THE MIRACLE ON GRASS

1950

When the U.S. national team entered the 1950 World Cup the hopes for a victory were not high. After two decades of decline, the sport had stagnated badly in the USA. The national team had participated in the 1948 Olympic Games but lost 9–0 in the first round against Italy. The results were similar in friendly games. For example, the team was defeated 11–0 by Norway. Oops!

A proper professional soccer league did not exist in the U.S. at the time, and the players were semi-professionals who had all kinds of other jobs in order to sustain themselves and their families.

Meanwhile, south of the border, Mexico was advancing in strides. In the North American qualification competition before the 1934 World Cup, the U.S. secured a confident victory over Mexico, but this time around, Mexico won two games,

totaling 12–2. By defeating Cuba, though, the U.S. also managed to qualify for the World Cup which was held in Brazil.

The North American Football Confederation took their time assembling a team and gathered players from all kinds of backgrounds up to the very last minute. For example, the Haitian Joe Gaetjens was called upon to join the team. He had at the time attracted attention for scoring goals in New York City but made a living by washing dishes at a restaurant. He wasn't an American citizen, but had applied for citizenship. According to regulations during that time, this was a sufficient criteria for playing with the U.S. national team.

The 1950 World Cup was the first time England had participated in the competition. Before the Brazilian World Cup, the

THE TEAM OF THE HISTORIC GAME AGAINST ENGLAND:

WALTER BAHR   FRANK WALLACE

HARRY KEOUGH

FRANK BORGHI   CHARLIE COLUMBO   GINO PARIANI

JOE GAETJENS

JOE MACA   JOHN SOUZA

ED MCILVENNY   ED SOUZA

John Souza of Massachusetts was named to the World Cup all-star team after the competition. Souza (1920–2012) is considered one of the most skilled soccer players the U.S. has as yet produced.

native land of soccer had refused to take part, but now most people expected an easy victory for the English team. Up until then, they had remained nearly invincible and many world famous players were on the team. As luck would have it, the fragile U.S. team ended up in the same group as England, and with this any optimism in regard to the U.S. team diminished even further.

That is, with everyone except the players themselves. The team had somehow managed to fill themselves with such confidence and bravado, that when the competition began, the team played well above their abilities.

In the first game against a dynamic Spanish team, the Americans had a surprising 1–0 lead until only 10 minutes remained. Gino Pariani from St. Louis had scored in the 17th minute, following which the U.S. team played a heroic defense. But after a late equalizer by the Spanish team, the U.S. defense collapsed and the Spanish swiftly added two more goals. However, everyone agreed that the U.S. team had played with surprising skill.

And so, a few days later, the American players met the English team with their heads held high.

This historic game was played in the city of Belo Horizonte, almost 250 miles north of Rio de Janeiro. The crowd numbered around 10,000 and they all supported the U.S., because the Brazilians wanted the powerful English team out of the competition as quickly as possible, so their own team would have a better chance of seizing the championship title.

And when the game began, the U.S. team's fighting spirit and determination aroused such admiration, that the crowd cheered for the underdogs with passion and energy.

The English team was so sure of its victory that they kept a few of their strongest players on the bench, and still anticipated something like a 10 goal victory. But early on, the U.S. defense showed that it was not going to be an easy win for the English. The defense was led by the confident 29-year-old Charlie Colombo from St. Louis. Colombo played a very rough game but got away with it. The goalkeeper Frank Borghi (also from St. Louis) also performed spectacularly. The few English shots that Borghi or Colombo and other U.S. defenders missed all seemed to hit the posts. The English offense just couldn't find the net while the U.S. team's fighting spirit and boldness grew as the game went on.

The Americans also had a few shots at the goal. 37 minutes into the game, Walter Bahr from Philadelphia shot the ball towards the goal. The English goalkeeper Bert Williams prepared to defend it, and it appeared he was going to have no trouble with it. Then, all of a sudden, Joe Gaetjens threw himself forward and touched the ball slightly with his head so that it changed its course. Williams had no time to react—except watch as the ball rolled into the net.

The English had plenty of opportunities to equalize the game but they simply couldn't manage. As the game rolled on the crowd grew, due to an overexcited

The US team. Back row from left: Jack Lyons, Joe Maca, Charlie Colombo, Frank Borghi, Harry Keogh, coach Bill Jeffrey. Front row, from left: Frank Wallace, Ed McIlvenny (captain), Gino Parlani, Joe Gaetjens, John "Clarkie" Souza, Ed Souza.

Brazilian radio announcer who encouraged people to come and witness the incredible tenacity of the U.S. team.

When the game was over the unheralded Americans had won one the most surprising victories in the history of the World Cup, even to this day. The results were so unexpected, that when the 1–0 U.S. victory over England reached the media around the world, people were convinced that the score was a typo, and the actual results had to be 10–1 in England's favor, or maybe 11–1. The game has been dubbed "the Miracle on Grass" ever since. The Americans were unfortunately unable to continue along the same lines. They started badly against Chile, who scored two early goals. By sheer persistence the U.S. managed to equalize the game at 2–2 but at that point the boundless energy of the team finally dried up and the Chileans scored three further goals before the game ended. The Americans had to pack their bags, but left Brazil with pride. The English team was also forced to return home, and in a very sullen mood. Shattered after the results against the U.S. team, they then lost to Spain, and were out of the World Cup.

Sadly, the heroic performance of the U.S. team was not enough to reverse the development of soccer in the country. 40 years would pass until the U.S. played in the World Cup finals again.

WORLD CUP 1950
Brazil

Date	Opponent	Result	U.S. Goals
6-25-50	Spain	1–3 ○	Pariani
6-29-50	England	1–0 ○	Gaetjens
7-2-50	Chile	2–6 ○	Wallace, Maca (p)

IV CAMPEONATO
MUNDIAL DE
FUTEBOL
·TAÇA JULES RIMET·

JUNHO DE 1950
BRASIL

THE HERO WHO DISAPPEARED

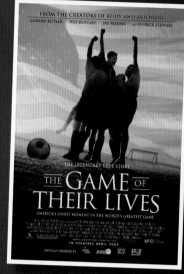

In the 2005 film, The Game of Their Lives, about the US game against England, Joe Gaetjens was depicted as a voodoo practitioner, much to the dismay of his family. In fact, Gaetjens was a Catholic.

Joe Gaetjens did not receive American citizenship, despite his famous goal. He eventually returned to Haiti and played one game with the Haitian national team.

Gaetjens was a withdrawn and humble but also an amiable man. His goal against England is often considered "lucky," but in fact Gaetjens was famous for scoring acrobatic goals and his teammates asserted that luck had nothing to do with his goal.

In 1964, the iron-fisted dictator of Haiti, Papa Doc Duvalier, began to increasingly tighten the leash of his countrymen. Gaetjens's family opposed his rule and fled the country, but Gaetjens saw no reason to join them. The dictator would hardly harm him, he claimed, since he was "only an athlete." Things turned out differently. Gaetjens was arrested and murdered by Duvalier's infamous secret police. His body was never found. It was a harrowing and sad end for the hero of the Belo Horizonte game.

In 1976, Gaetjens' honor was restored posthumously, when he was inducted into the United States National Soccer Hall of Fame.

English goalkeeper Bert Williams and Joe Gaetjens.

"THE SHOT HEARD ROUND THE WORLD"

The years following the 1950 World Cup were sad times for the U.S. national team. At home, the league competition was not much to speak of and the national team felt the consequences. Further World Cup finals were clearly out of reach and the team even lost friendly games against minnows like Iceland (1955), and Israel and Bermuda (1973). Friendlies against England (1959 and 1964) now concluded with "natural" results, according to the English, who won 8–1 and 10–0. The performance of the U.S. team in matchups with Mexico was also sobering. The U.S. won the first game between the teams in 1934, but then the Mexicans won the next 10 games in a row. In a total of 24 games up until 1980, the Mexican team defeated the U.S. 21 times. Three games ended with a tie. In 1968, a new and ambitious league was established in the United States and Canada, which was named the North American Soccer League. For a time, the managers of the league successfully harnessed the U.S.'s underlying interest in soccer. Audience numbers multiplied as people flocked to stadiums to watch truly exciting and well-played matches. Established stars from Europe and South America joined ambitious teams such as the New York Cosmos, Chicago Sting, Los Angeles Aztecs, and others.

This state of affairs did not immediately impact the U.S. national team. For the time being it seldom managed to attract the attention of the public. More people attended college games than showed up for the national team. And things carried on downhill; the team lost 12 consecutive games from October 1973 to August 1975. Sadly, the NASL had not been built on sturdy foundations and the league folded in 1984.

Nevertheless, signs of progress for the national team finally began to emerge. The strings of losses decreased and strong players appeared here and there, across the United States. Finally, on November 23, 1980, an amazing thing occurred. In a 1982 World Cup qualification match in Fort Lauderdale, Florida, the U.S. stunned everyone by beating Mexico for the first time in 46 years. Steve Moyers from St. Louis scored both goals in a 2–1 win. The victory was not enough to win the U.S. a place in the 1982 World Cup finals, but it did set new standards. The U.S. team has since had the upper hand in their long-standing rivalry with Mexico.

On November 19, 1989, the long-awaited moment finally arrived, which American soccer fans had hoped for almost 40 years. The CONCACAF Championship that year was also a qualification competition for the 1990 World Cup in Italy. The U.S. team competed with Trinidad and Tobago for a place in the World Cup, and in order to qualify, had to win the last game against them in the capital of the Caribbean island nation. A tie would be enough for Trinidad and Tobago to proceed. In the 30th minute defensive midfielder Paul Caligiuri unleashed a 30-yard shot which proved the only goal of the match. The U.S. had finally earned a place among the world's elite. Caligiuri's fine goal was called the "the shot heard round the world." Suddenly the "beautiful game" of soccer seemed on the rise in the USA.

In 1989 Paul Caligiuri was playing for an undistinguished German team, SV Meppen. With his goal the U.S. team managed to get to the World Cup. Caligiuri was a fair but tough player and here he fouls the Italian Berti during the USA-Italy World Cup game in 1990.

Pelé who played for Brazil from 1958–1970, was the greatest player in the world and maybe the greatest player in history. He ended his career with the New York Cosmos 1975–1977, a sign of the great but ultimately unfullfilled ambition of the NASL.

BACK AMONG THE BEST

The U.S. team was rather hopeful prior to the 1990 World Cup in Italy. The U.S. had been awarded the chance to host the next World Cup in four years' time, so interest in soccer was on a steady rise in the country and a budding generation of powerful soccer players had emerged on the scene. Individuals such as Tony Meola, John Harkes, Tab Ramos, Eric Wynalda, Marcelo Balboa, Alexi Lalas, Brian Bliss, and Peter Vermes.

The performance in Italy unfortunately left a lot to be desired. In the first game against Czechoslovakia, the U.S. team was clearly out of its depth and crashed badly. To add insult to injury, the key player Wynalda was sent off the field early in the second half. Interestingly, the U.S. team's sole consolation goal was scored by the hero from the Trinidad game, Paul Caligiuri.

In the game against the strongest team in the group stage, however, the U.S. team was in their best form. Italy, three-time world champions, and playing at home, won a mere 1–0 victory with a goal early in the game. The U.S. team did not manage to build on that in their last game, so they headed home with three straight defeats, but were still happy. They had at least learned a lot and many aspects of the U.S. game seemed promising for the future.

THE WINNER IS ...

GERMANY

Defeated Argentina 1–0 in a tense gritty match.

WORLD CUP 1990
Italy

Date	Opponent	Result	U.S. Goals
6-10-90	Czechoslovakia	1–5 ○	Caligiuri
6-14-90	Italy	0–1 ○	
6-19-90	Austria	1–2 ○	Murray

Tough times for the U.S. in Italy. The home team's Gianluca Vialli battles with the USA's Desmond Armstrong.

THE WORLD CUP IN THE USA

1994

The 15th edition of the World Cup soccer finals was hosted by the USA in the summer of 1994. The choice of venue had met with a good deal of controversy, because the sport's greatest powerhouse, Brazil, had also made a bid for the finals. No one doubted the U.S.'s ability to host an extraordinary sporting event. However, many still considered the choice bad, given that soccer was not more popular in the United States. The U.S. didn't even have a national league competition. Some feared that the games would be played within half-empty stadiums due to the lack of interest in the sport.

Those who argued on the side of the U.S. claimed that hosting the competition would greatly boost the popularity of soccer in the country.

And as FIFA bosses had hoped to wake the "Sleeping Giant" from his slumber, the World Cup finally arrived in the U.S. in 1994.

The competition turned out to be a great success and the average attendance of 69,000 is still a World Cup record. Many great games were played and the competition was much livelier than fans had witnessed in the rather drab 1990 World Cup finals in Italy.

A new league was established in connection with the World Cup, Major League Soccer, which formally began two years later. This fact would most definitely enhance the performance of the U.S. team in future World Cup finals.

THE WINNER IS ...

 BRAZIL

After a goalless draw, Brazil beat Italy in a penalty shootout, the first time the World Cup had been decided in this manner.

Proud U.S. fans during the national team's first game against Switzerland.

U.S. goalkeeper and captain Tony Meola and defender Alexi Lalas combine to keep out Brazil's Marcio Santos. Lalas was an instantly recognizable figure in USA's defense from 1991–1998.

WORLD CUP 1994
United States

Date	Opponent	Result		U.S. Goals
6-18-94	Switzerland	1–1	○	Wynalda
6-22-94	Colombia	2–1	○	Escobar (o.g.), Stewart
6-26-94	Romania	0–1	○	
7-4-94	Brazil	0–1	○	

A WORTHY OPPONENT

An aerial view of the Rose Bowl in Pasadena, California during the 1994 World Cup Final.

The first game of the U.S. team in the 1994 World Cup finals was against Switzerland. The game took place in the Pontiac Silverdome near Detroit, and was first ever World Cup game to take place indoors. The Swiss scored a fine goal from a free kick, but Eric Wynalda equalized with an even more graceful free kick from 28 yards. After that, the U.S. defense was equal to anything the Swiss could throw at it in the second half. Then the U.S. team won an unanticipated victory over a highly volatile Colombian team, but lost its final preliminary group game against Romania in a stifling heat in Pasadena, California, where the game against Colombia also took place. The Romania game was witnessed by a crowd of 93,869 at the Rose Bowl in Pasadena and was a record breaker for soccer.

With three points in the group stage, the U.S. advanced from their group, but faced a challenging task—a match with the great Brazilians.

The World Cup had already stirred a never-before-seen level of interest in soccer in the U.S., and now, soccer passion had reached a fever pitch. And it didn't hurt that the game took place on the 4th of July. The game was played in the Stanford stadium in California.

As could be expected, the U.S. team struggled against the skillful Brazilians, led by super striker Romário, but the U.S. still defended with vigor.

It wasn't until the 72nd minute that Bebeto broke the ice and scored the only goal of the game. The American players were out of the finals but everyone agreed that the team had performed quite well, in fact, much better than most could have hoped for.

The team has proven that the USA was becoming a worthy competitor for even the strongest soccer nations.

ROUGH!

In the game between Brazil and the United States, the Brazilian defender Leonardo harshly elbowed the U.S. midfielder Tab Ramos, leaving the American with a fractured skull. Ramos had been playing very well in the game. Leonardo was immediately suspended which meant that Brazil was one player short for more than 40 minutes. Unfortunately, the U.S. couldn't take advantage of that. Leonardo later apologized profusely and Ramos eventually recovered.

A TRAGIC END!

The match between the U.S. and Colombia in the second leg of the group stage ended well for the U.S. but became a tragedy for the Colombians. They entered the World Cup highly optimistic about their chances and some believed they might even win the gold medal.

Their top players included the explosive striker Faustino Asprilla, the powerful midfielder Freddy Rincón, and the elegant Carlos Valderrama, famous for his blonde Afro hairdo.

The Colombians unexpectedly lost to Romania in the first group game and then the U.S. team took everyone by surprise and beat Colombia 2–1 in the next game. It was then clear that the Colombians would return home with their tails between their legs. The first U.S. goal was an awkward own goal, which the Colombian defender Andrés Escobar scored. Less than two weeks after the game, Escobar was shot to death in his home city, Medellín, in Colombia. The murder was seen as some kind of retaliation for the own goal.

Andrés Escobar of Colombia tries to control the ball during Colombia's 1–2 loss to the USA in a match at the Rose Bowl in Pasadena.

DISAPPOINTMENT IN FRANCE

1998

The U.S. team was in positive spirits when it entered the 1998 World Cup in France. The team had shown great strength and energy during the long and tough qualification campaign and had played well in the Gold Cup in February (see page 44). The U.S. team also played promisingly in friendly games: just before the competition began, FIFA ranked the U.S. at number 11 on the list of the strongest soccer nations in the world. Despite the controversy about the FIFA ranking system, this clearly showed that the U.S. team had grown over the previous decade.

However, when push came to shove, the U.S. team played poorly and lost all its games. Losing to Germany was natural enough, since the Germans always field an extremely strong team. Jürgen Klinsmann, the U.S. team's current head coach, scored the second goal of the game. In the game against Iran, though, the U.S. team never seemed to hit form, simply played badly, and was already eliminated after only two games. The third game offered no consolation.

It turned out that there had been much tension and conflict in the U.S. team between coach Steve Sampson and a number of key players of the team. These conflicts influenced the morale and fighting spirit of the team and played their part in how things turned out. Following the tournament in France, Sampson resigned and Bruce Arena replaced him.

Claudio Reyna (number 21) celebrates the only goal the U.S. scored in France. Midfielder Reyna had great success as a player in Europe. He was the first American to captain a European team (Wolfsburg in Germany) and also played for Rangers in Scotland and Sunderland and Manchester

WORLD CUP 1998
France

Date	Opponent	Result	U.S. Goal
6-15-98	Germany	0–2 ⚪	

SOCCER AND POLITICS

The game between the U.S. and Iran was highly significant because for almost two decades the relationship of the two countries had been characterized by bitter political differences. On the soccer field, however, the rival teams showed each other the utmost civility.

It is interesting to note that earlier in the year, during the Gold Cup competition, the U.S. team for the first time (in a very long while) played against another team whose nation the U.S. was on unfavorable political terms with. The country was Cuba. The U.S. and Cuba hadn't played each other since 1959.

THE WINNER IS ...

 FRANCE

Defeated the defending champions Brazil surprisingly easily 3–0.

SURPRISE IN ASIA

2002

The U.S. team's path toward the 2002 World Cup, hosted by South Korea and Japan, was not an entirely smooth one. Surprisingly, Costa Rica dominated the CONCACAF qualification competition and the U.S. had to wait until the second-to-last round to clinch third spot and ultimately a place in the World Cup finals.

When the competition began, fans of the U.S. team were not sure what they could expect. Many of the team's players were quite experienced, but there were also a few promising young men on the team, such as the 20-year-old Landon Donovan from California. Roughly half the team played in Europe, most with powerful teams, but the other half played with teams in the newly established American professional league, Major League Soccer. The MLS was proving its worth as a popular avenue for soccer in the United States.

Expectations were low at the start of the first game when the U.S. faced Portugal. Cristiano Ronaldo had not begun playing with the Portuguese national team, but the team was still filled with great players, who played elegant and fast soccer. But the U.S. team showed no undue respect and took everyone completely by surprise by reaching 3–0 before the Portuguese finally hit their stride. In the end, Portugal only managed to reduce the difference to one goal just before the end of the game. The result delighted the U.S. fans, after all, it's not every day that the U.S. team is able to defeat one of Europe's strongest teams. The victory was fully deserved.

In the next round, the U.S. team's game with the aggressive South Korean team ended with a draw, but in the third round they lost to the Polish team. The proud Poles had already been eliminated, but they were going to leave with a bang, and they surely did. As it was, other results turned out to be favorable to the U.S. team, so they went on to the knockout phase.

John O'Brien (number 5) fires in the first goal of the USA–Portugal match. O'Brien (born 1977 in LA) was a defensive midfielder and one of the first Americans to earn a starting spot with a major European team, with Ajax Amsterdam in the Netherlands. Injuries put an end to his highly promising career.

It just so happened that in the knockout phase the U.S. confronted their eternal rivals, the Mexicans. The time when Mexico could count on an easy triumph over their neighbors to the north, was now ancient history. Bruce Arena's team took the lead when the sharpshooting Brian McBride powered the ball into the net, following a clever build-up by Claudio Reyna and Josh Wolff. The Mexican team was thrown off balance and late in the game, Donovan headed the ball into the goal after a precise cross from Eddie Lewis. The U.S. team, who had been such an easy prey for the world's strongest teams only two decades before, had now made it into the quarterfinals of the World Cup and could thus count themselves among the eight strongest teams on the globe.

Their next opponents on the other hand were no weaklings. The Germans were as powerful as always. Michael Ballack, one of the world's leading midfielders at that time, scored in the 39th minute. The Americans threw everything into a desperate attack but the German defense and the great goalkeeper Oliver Kahn withstood all attacks, and eventually sent the U.S. team packing. But this time, there was general consensus that the U.S. team had played skillful and attractive soccer and earned a well-deserved success.

The U.S. team's captain, Claudio Reyna, became only the third American (after Bert Patenaude in 1930 and John Souza in 1950) to be named to the World Cup all-star team.

WORLD CUP 2002
Japan/South Korea

Date	Opponent	Result	U.S. Goals
6-5-02	Portugal	3–2 ○	O'Brien, Costa (o.g.), McBride
6-10-02	South Korea	1–1 ◉	Mathis
6-14-02	Poland	1–3 ○	Donovan
6-17-02	Mexico	2–0 ○	McBride, Donovan
6-21-02	Germany	0–1 ○	

Powerful German defender Christoph Metzelder of Borussia Dortmund falls under the challenge from U.S. youngster Landon Donovan during the USA-Germany World Cup match.

THE WINNER IS ...

BRAZIL

For the record-breaking fifth time. They defeated Germany 2–0 with two goals from the original Ronaldo.

U.S. fans celebrating during the game against Mexico.

MISERY IN GERMANY

2006

The U.S. comfortably entered the 2006 World Cup in Germany by winning the CONCACAF qualifying tournament after a tough scuffle with Mexico. Everyone seemed to agree that a stronger team was now headed off to the World Cup in Germany than had played in South Korea and Japan four years earlier, so this time the expectations were high. The U.S. landed in a difficult group, however, which included the three-time world champions of Italy, and the Czech Republic, who had an extremely strong national team at the time. In addition, the team from Ghana was powerful and unpredictable.

But the U.S. team believed they had good reason for optimism. Just two months prior to the World Cup finals, a new FIFA rating list revealed that the United States was in fourth place of all the world's national teams!

As it turned out, everything went wrong. The U.S. team never managed to get into shape against the fierce Czechs and were lucky to escape with only a three-goal loss.

Landon Donovan of the USA battles for the ball with Gennaro Gattuso of Italy during the FIFA World Cup Germany 2006 Group E match between Italy and USA at the Fritz-Walter Stadium on June 17, 2006, in Kaiserslautern, Germany.

WORLD CUP 2006
Germany

Date	Opponent	Result	U.S. Goals
6-12-06	Czech Republic	0–3 ○	
6-17-06	Italy	1–1 ○	Zaccardo (o.g.)
6-22-06	Ghana	1–2 ○	Dempsey

In the game against Italy, the U.S. team seemed determined to get into form but then the Italians scored. Shortly after, the Italians scored an own goal and the game seemed to be going in a more positive direction, especially since the Italian team had lost a player due to a red card. But the U.S. team didn't manage to make use of their opponent's player deficit. Before the game was over the U.S. had lost two of their own players, and they could count themselves lucky with a draw.

It was clear that if the U.S. team could defeat Ghana, they would proceed to the knockout stage, but unfortunately they failed to achieve this. The Ghana team showed great fighting spirit and even though the Americans gave it all they had, the team was lacking the imagination and tactics needed to beat the spirited African team. Because of the loss, the U.S. team was the least successful of all the 32 teams in the competition. This was a great blow to the Americans, and consequently, Bruce Arena's contract was not renewed.

THE WINNER IS ...

 **ITALY**

Defeated France in penalty shoot-out after a tense 1–1 draw in regular time.

FIFA World Ranking
April 2006

Rank	Team	Points
1	Brazil	830
2	Czech Republic	779
3	Netherlands	774
4	USA	760
5	Spain	759
6	Mexico	758
7	France	754
8	Portugal	753
9	Argentina	753
10	England	744

This performance would once have been considered amazing: the USA in fourth place on the FIFA ratings list. The calculations of the rating system were later changed at which point the U.S. automatically tumbled to a lower position on the list.

2010

UP AGAINST ENGLAND, AGAIN

Clint Dempsey clashing with legendary English midfielder Steven Gerrard during the U.S. opening game against England. Incredibly, the U.S. finished ahead of England in the group stage.

36

WORLD CUP 2010
South Africa

Date	Opponent	Result	U.S. Goals
6-12-10	England	1–1 ⬤	Dempsey
6-18-10	Slovenia	2–2 ⬤	Donovan, Bradley
6-23-10	Algeria	1–0 ⬤	Donovan
6-23-10	Ghana	1–2* ⬤	Donovan (p)

* After extra time.

Bob Bradley led his team with ease through the CONCACAF qualification tournament for the 2010 World Cup finals in South Africa. There was only one problem; the goals seemed a bit hard to come by. Hopes were high, however, that the performance of the explosive youngster Jozy Altidore of New Jersey would complement experienced goal-getters like Landon Donovan and Clint Dempsey. Donovan was still only 28 years old but had amassed an incredible total of 123 international games, with 42 goals, before the World Cup finals began.

The U.S. team landed in a relatively manageable preliminary group, so there were strong hopes that the team would make it into the knockout stage, and advance even further than in 2002. An interesting opponent awaited them in the first game—England. The game attracted much attention, not least because of memories from the 1950 World Cup, and tensions were high. The game began badly for the U.S. team, with English team captain Steven Gerrard's goal in the 4th minute.

The U.S. team then got lucky when English goalkeeper Robert Green fumbled a seemingly harmless shot by Dempsey. The ball somehow crept into the net in the 40th minute. In the second half, neither team managed to add goals in spite of many chances. U.S. goalkeeper Tim Howard was chosen the man of the match for his great performance in this entertaining game.

In the next game, the U.S. team was two goals behind against Slovenia, but finally caught their stride and equalized. In their next game, the U.S. team had to wait into stoppage time before Donovan, with his fighting spirit, scored the winning goal against the tenacious Algerians. Due to fortunate results in other games in the competition, two draws and a win were enough for the U.S. team to win their group—ahead of England!

In the knockout phase, the Americans faced Ghana, just like they had four years earlier. 13 million Americans watched the game on TV which proved that interest in soccer was still rising. The Ghana team was off to a better start, but Donovan equalized with his third goal in the competition. Despite several opportunities, neither team managed to score again, until in extra time, when the Ghana team secured their victory in a hard-fought game.

THE WINNER IS ...

 SPAIN

Defeated the Netherlands 1–0 after extra time.

THE COACHES

THOMAS CAHILL (1864–1951) was the first coach of the national team. He was one of the founding fathers of soccer in the U.S. and steered the team in two games in 1916, winning the first and drawing the second.
1916

BOB MILLAR (1889–1967) was born in Scotland and started his football career there with St. Mirren. In 1911 he emigrated to America and played with over a dozen teams in at least five U.S. leagues. While playing for Bethlehem Steel in 1914–15 he scored a record 59 goals in 34 games. Millar retired as a New York Giants player in 1929. By then he was already U.S. coach and managed the team during the highly successful 1930 World Cup.
1930

BILL JEFFREY (1892–1966) was also born in Scotland but emigrated to the U.S. as a young man. He coached the Penn State soccer team for 26 years, winning 10 national championships along the way. He was chosen as the national team coach just two weeks before the 1950 World Cup in Brazil.
1950

BOB GANSLER (B. 1941) was born in Hungary. He played five games for the U.S. national team in 1968. In 1990 he led the U.S. national team to its first World Cup appearance in 40 years.
1989–1991

BORA MILUTINOVIČ (B. 1944) was born in Serbia and played for various reasonably strong European teams as a player. He then started an immensly successful coaching career and has coached five different national teams at the World Cup: Mexico in 1986, Costa Rica in 1990, the U.S. in 1994, Nigeria in 1998, and China in 2002. Altogether he has coached eight national teams.
1991–1995

STEVE SAMPSON (B. 1957) was young and energetic when he brought an experienced U.S. team to the 1998 World Cup in France. Expectations were high but the team crashed out of the competition with three losses, for example, losing to Iran in a tense encounter.
1995–1998

Steve Sampson during a visit to the Eiffel Tower in Paris, France, during the USA World Cup training, on June 14, 1998.

Bruce Arena.

Bob Bradley.

Bill Jeffrey.

BRUCE ARENA (B. 1951) led the national team to its greatest success at the World Cup in 2002 when the U.S. reached the quarterfinals. Four years later, however, he seemed to have lost his touch, and was severly criticized for the team's below-par performance in Germany's 2006 World Cup.
1998–2006

BOB BRADLEY (B. 1958) showed that recent results were no fluke when he led the U.S. to second place in the 2009 Confederations Cup, where his team ended a 35-game unbeaten run—and a 15 game winning streak—by European Champions Spain by beating them 2–0. This was followed by the top spot in a tough World Cup group in World Cup 2010. After a period of lackluster results Bradley was fired in 2011.
2006–2011

KLINSMANN

Head Coach from 2011–Present

Jürgen Klinsmann was born on July 30, 1964, in a small town in Germany. He began his famed professional career as a scorer with teams in Stuttgart, after which he moved to Inter Milan in Italy, and then on to Monaco in the French leading division. He also played with, among others, Tottenham in England and giants Bayern Munich in his home country. Klinsmann finished his career by playing— first using a pseudonym—with the small California team Blue Star in Orange County.

Wherever Klinsmann played soccer, he scored a lot of goals and gained popularity for his daring offensive play, passion, and optimism.

He became world champion with the German national team in 1990, European champion in 1996, and won the U.S. Cup in 1993. Klinsmann scored a total of 47 goals in 108 national games from 1987 to 1998.

In 2004, Klinsmann was unexpectedly chosen as head coach for the German national team. The national team had long been considered tedious, known for playing a defensive and even dull game. The team was practically unbeatable, but at the same time both not impressive and unpopular. However, when Klinsmann took over the team, everything changed.

The character of the German players seemed to change almost overnight, and they became known for their newfound passion and attacking flair. Klinsmann left a definite mark on the German national team even though he only coached them for three years.

Klinsmann was named head coach of the U.S. team in July 2011. In the first few games, the results were so-so, but when Klinsmann's team defeated the four-time world champion, Italy, 1–0 on February 29, 2012, it became clear that things were improving. Clint Dempsey scored the winning goal. On August 15, in the same year, the U.S. defeated its long standing rival, Mexico, in a friendly game in the Azteca Stadium in Mexico City. Michael Orozco scored the only goal, making it the first time the U.S. had defeated Mexico in this famous stadium, a stronghold of Mexican soccer.

Then, on June 2, 2013, Klinsmann led his team to a famous 4–3 victory over Germany in a centennial commemorative game. Jozy Altidore's goal opened the scoring for the U.S., Clint Dempsey added two more goals, and the fourth was an own goal. In the same year, Klinsmann won the Gold Cup with the U.S. team (see page 49.)

On September 10, 2013, the U.S. secured qualification for the 2014 World Cup in Brazil with a 2–0 victory over Mexico.

Now, Klinsmann's team will travel to Brazil, bursting with confidence and spirit.

Landon Donovan is embraced by Jürgen Klinsmann after coming off against Guatemala at Qualcomm Stadium on July 5, 2013, in San Diego, California.

Klinsmann celebrates becoming World Champion when his team defeated Argentina in the 1990 World Cup final.

WINNING STREAK!

The USA's victory over Germany in Washington D.C. on June 2, 2013, began a record-breaking winning-streak for the U.S. team. Altogether, the USA won 12 games, an interesting contrast with the 12 lost games from 1973–75, see page 20! This remarkable run finally came to an end, when the team was defeated by Costa Rica on September 6th.

Date	Opponent	Competition	Result	
6-2-13	Germany	Friendly	4–3	○
6-7-13	Jamaica	World Cup Qualification	2–1	○
6-11-13	Panama	World Cup Qualification	2–0	○
6-18-13	Honduras	World Cup Qualification	1–0	○
7-5-13	Guatemala	Friendly	6–0	○
7-9-13	Belize	Gold Cup	6–1	○
7-13-13	Cuba	Gold Cup	4–1	○
7-16-13	Costa Rica	Gold Cup	1–0	○
7-21-13	El Salvador	Gold Cup	5–1	○
7-24-13	Honduras	Gold Cup	3–1	○
7-28-13	Panama	Gold Cup	1–0	○
8-14-13	Bosnia-Herzegovina	Friendly	4–3	○

FIVE GOLD CUPS!

CANADA
35,236,000

The U.S. Soccer Federation is a member of CONCACAF, the Confederation of North, Central American, and Caribbean Association Football. Since 1963, the confederation has organized a championship comparable to UEFA's European Championship and South America's Copa América. Since 1991 the championship has been called the Gold Cup.

UNITED STATES
316,102,000

The U.S. team first played in the qualifying competition for the CONCACAF championship in 1969 but only managed to reach the final competition in 1985. Since then the U.S. has played in all the competitions and won the Gold Cup five times.

Besides teams from CONCACAF, guest teams from other federations (mainly South America) have occasionally been invited as guests.

CUBA
11,164,000

BELIZE
340,000

JAMAICA
2,715,000

HONDURAS
8,578,000

HAITI
10,671,000

GUADELOUPE 409,000

MARTINIQUE 398,000

TRINIDAD & TOBAGO
1,346,350

The USA and its opponents in CONCACAF Gold Cup finals. The numbers indicate population in 2013.

BRAZIL
201,032,000

PERU
30,475,000

CONCACAF Championship 1985

Date	Opponent	Result		U.S. Goals
5-15-85	Trinidad & Tobago	2–1	○	Borja, Peterson
5-19-85	Trinidad & Tobago	1–0	○	Caligiuri
5-26-85	Costa Rica	1–1	◐	Kerr
5-31-85	Costa Rica	0–1	○	

Canada won the championship.

CONCACAF Championship 1989

Date	Opponent	Result		U.S. Goals
4-16-89	Costa Rica	0–1	○	
4-30-89	Costa Rica	1–0	○	Ramos
5-13-89	Trinidad & Tobago	1–1	◐	Trittschuh
6-17-89	Guatemala	2–1	○	Murray, Eichmann
9-17-89	El Salvador	1–0	○	Perez
10-8-89	Guatemala	0–0	◐	
11-5-89	El Salvador	0–0	◐	
11-19-89	Trinidad & Tobago	1–0	○	Caligiuri

USA and Costa Rica shared first place. Costa Rica became champion on goal difference. The U.S. couldn't care less as the results of the last game got their team to the 1990 World Cup finals.

CONCACAF Gold Cup 1991

Date	Opponent	Result		U.S. Goals
6-29-91	Trinidad & Tobago	2–1	○	Murray, Balboa
7-1-91	Guatemala	3–0	○	Murray, Quinn, Wynalda
7-3-91	Costa Rica	3–2	○	Vermes, Perez (p), Marchena (o.g.)
7-5-91	Mexico	2–0	○	Doyle, Vermes
7-7-91	Honduras	0–0 (4–3*)	○	

* After extra time and penalty shootout.

USA defeated Honduras in the final in a penalty shootout. Neither the U.S. nor Honduras performed particularly well in the shootout, as a total of 8 rounds were needed to get a result. This win truly put the U.S. on the international soccer map. The team had obviously made tremendous progress in a short time under new coach Milutinovic (see page 38.)

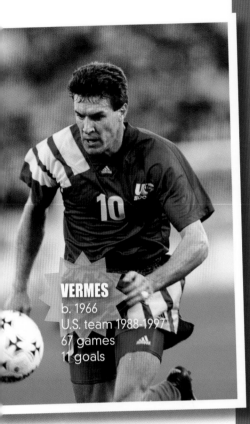

VERMES
b. 1966
U.S. team 1988-1997
67 games
11 goals

Peter Vermes, a native of New Jersey, captained the U.S. team to its first Gold Cup win. He then played as a striker but later distinguished himself as a defender. Vermes played for many teams in the U.S., including the Colorado Rapids and Kansas City Wizards.

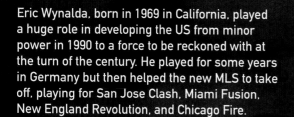

Eric Wynalda, born in 1969 in California, played a huge role in developing the US from minor power in 1990 to a force to be reckoned with at the turn of the century. He played for some years in Germany but then helped the new MLS to take off, playing for San Jose Clash, Miami Fusion, New England Revolution, and Chicago Fire.

CONCACAF Gold Cup 1993
United States and Mexico

Date	Opponent	Result	U.S. Goals
7-10-93	Jamaica	1–0 ○	Wynalda
7-14-93	Panama	2–1 ○	Wynalda, Dooley
7-17-93	Honduras	1–0 ○	Lalas
7-22-93	Costa Rica	1–0* ○	Kooiman
7-25-93	Mexico	0–4 ○	

* After extra time.
Mexico won the Gold Cup, beating the U.S. convincingly in a final in the Azteca Stadium in Mexico City.

CONCACAF Gold Cup 1996
United States

Date	Opponent	Result		U.S. Goals
1-13-96	Trinidad & Tobabo	3–2	●	Wynalda 2, Moore
1-16-96	El Salvador	2–0	●	Wynalda, Balboa
1-18-96	Brazil	0–1	●	
1-21-96	Guatemala	3–0	●	Wynalda, Agoos, Kirovski

USA won the bronze medal by beating Guatemala. Mexico won the Gold Cup by beating guests Brazil in Los Angeles Memorial Coliseum. Eric Wynalda was the top scorer with 4 goals.

CONCACAF Gold Cup 1998
United States

Date	Opponent	Result		U.S. Goals
2-1-98	Cuba	3–0	●	Wegerle, Wynalda, Moore (p)
2-7-98	Costa Rica	2–1	●	Pope, Preki
2-10-98	Brazil	1–0	●	Preki
2-15-98	Mexico	0–1	●	

The U.S. made soccer history by defeating world champions Brazil, for the first time. Brazil played as guests in the competition and were fielding a very strong team with Romário and Edmundo in attack, Zinho and Júnior in midfield, and Taffarel in goal. The U.S. goalkeeper Kasey Keller was the hero of the day (see page 50.) Unfortunately this historic win didn't help the U.S. in the final, which Mexico won.

CONCACAF Gold Cup 2000
United States

Date	Opponent	Result		U.S. Goals
2-12-00	Haiti	3–0	●	Kirovski, Wynalda (p), Jones
2-16-00	Peru	1–0	●	Jones
2-19-00	Colombia*	2–2* (1–2)	●	McBride, Armas

The U.S. lost in the quarterfinals to Colombia (*after extra time) and penalties. Eddie Lewis was the only one of five U.S. players who scored from the spot. Canada recorded the country's greatest achievement in soccer by beating Colombia in the final, having already sent Mexico packing.

CONCACAF Gold Cup 2002

United States

Date	Opponent	Result		U.S. Goals
1-19-02	South Korea	2–1	○	Donovan, Beasley
1-21-02	Cuba	1–0	○	McBride
1-27-02	El Salvador	4–0	○	McBride 3, Razov
1-30-02	Canada	0–0* (4–2*)	○	
2-2-02	Costa Rica	2–0	○	Wolff, Agoos

* After extra time and penalties.

The U.S. team played well and won the Gold Cup for the second time. Brian McBride recorded the first hat trick an American player had scored in a major tournament since 1930 (see page 14.) His four goals made him top scorer. The final was played in the Rose Bowl in Pasadena.

CONCACAF Gold Cup 2003

United States and Mexico

Date	Opponent	Result		U.S. Goals
7-12-03	El Salvador	2–0	○	Lewis, McBride
7-14-03	Martinique	2–0	○	McBride 2
7-19-03	Cuba	5–0	○	Donovan 4, Ralston
7-23-03	Brazil	1–2*	○	Bocanegra
7-26-03	Costa Rica	3–2	○	Bocanegra, Stewart, Convey

* After extra time.

Brian McBride and Landon Donovan ran rampant in the early stages, but in the semifinal game against Brazil, Kesey Keller couldn't quite repeat his heroics of five years earlier. The Brazilian world champions had to wait for a penalty deep into extra time to finally see off the spirited Americans. The U.S. team then defeated Costa Rica in a match for third place.

CONCACAF Gold Cup 2005

United States

Date	Opponent	Result		U.S. Goals
7-7-05	Cuba	4–1	○	Dempsey, Donovan 2, Beasley
7-9-05	Canada	2–0	○	Hutchinson (o.g.), Donovan
7-12-05	Costa Rica	0–0	●	
7-16-05	Jamaica	3–1	●	Wolff, Beasley 2
7-21-05	Honduras	2–1	●	O'Brien, Onyewu
7-24-05	Panama	0–0* (3–1*)	●	

* After extra time and penalties.

Many of the regular starters for the U.S. team were missing for this edition of the Gold Cup. In spite of this, the team had a relatively easy ride to the final, but then couldn't overcome stubborn Panama and had to rely on the penalty shootout.

CONCACAF Gold Cup 2007

United States

Date	Opponent	Result		U.S. Goals
6-7-07	Guatemala	1–0	○	Dempsey
6-9-07	Trinidad & Tobago	2–0	○	Ching, E. Johnson
6-12-07	El Salvador	4–0	○	Beasley 2, Donovan (p), Twellman
6-16-07	Panama	2–1	○	Donovan (p), Bocanegra
6-21-07	Canada	2–1	○	Hejduk, Donovan (p)

USA won for the second time running by playing with confidence and power. Mexico took the lead in the final but two second-half goals secured the fourth win for the U.S. Donovan was the top scorer on the U.S. team, interestingly scoring all four of his goals from the penalty spot.

CONCACAF Gold Cup 2009

United States

Date	Opponent	Result	U.S. Goals
7-4-09	Grenada	4–0 ○	F. Adu, Holden, Rogers, Davies
7-8-09	Honduras	2–0 ○	Quaranta, Ching
7-11-09	Haiti	2–2 ◉	Arnaud, Holden
7-18-09	Panama	2–1* ○	Beckerman, Cooper (p)
7-23-09	Honduras	2–0 ○	Goodson, Cooper
7-26-09	Mexico	0–5 ○	

* After extra time.

The U.S. showed up with a second-string team, which advanced easily to the final. In the first half the Americans held their own against a strong Mexican team but in the second half everything collapsed. The silver medal was slight consolation after 5 goals in 35 minutes. This was the first time in 10 years that USA had lost to Mexico on home soil.

Donovan was ruthless from the penalty spot during the 2007 Gold Cup.

CONCACAF Gold Cup 2011

United States

Date	Opponent	Result	U.S. Goals
6-7-11	Canada	2–0 ○	Altidore, Dempsey
6-11-11	Panama	1–2 ○	Goodson
6-14-11	Guadeloupe	1–0 ○	Altidore
6-19-11	Jamaica	2–0 ○	Jones, Dempsey
6-22-11	Panama	1–0 ○	Dempsey
6-25-11	Mexico	2–4 ○	Bradley, Donovan

The U.S., with a much stronger team than two years earlier, advanced safely to the final, in spite of a setback against Panama in the group stage. In the final the U.S. seemed all set to take the game by the horns and scored two goals in the first 23 minutes. But the sprightly Mexicans equalized before the break, and then scored two more in the second half.

CONCACAF Gold Cup 2013

United States

Date	Opponent	Result	US Goals
7-9-13	Belize	6–1 ○	Wondolowski 3, Holden, Orozco, Donovan (p)
7-13-13	Cuba	4–1 ○	Donovan (p), Corona, Wondolowski 2
7-16-13	Costa Rica	1–0 ○	Shea
7-21-13	El Salvador	5–1 ○	Goodson, Corona, E. Johnson, Donovan, Diskerud
7-24-13	Honduras	3–1 ○	E. Johnson, Donovan 2
7-28-13	Panama	1–0 ○	Shea

The new coach Jürgen Klinsmann started well, comfortably winning the USA its fifth Gold Cup. The team was never in trouble and scored a lot of goals, which showed how offensive-minded Klinsmann is. Much to the USA's chagrin Panama defeated Mexico in the semifinals and thus the US didn't get to retaliate after the results of the last two Gold Cup finals. The final against Panama was rather subdued and the U.S. only scored in the 69th minute when substitute Brek Shea netted 42 seconds after coming on the field.

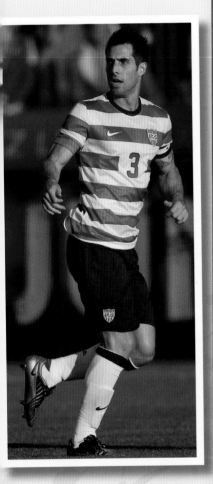

Carlos Bocanegra hails from California and has been a defensive stalwart on the U.S. team since 2001. This hardworking and dependable center back has played for various European teams. He has also scored a number of important goals for the U.S. team.

BEATING ARGENTINA

The U.S. has played three times as a guest in Copa América, the South American equivalent of the CONCACAF Gold Cup. In 1993 and 2007 the going was tough and the U.S. had to be satisfied with the last place in its premilinary group.

The 1995 edition was a different story altogether. The U.S. was then considered the underdog among some very strong South American teams, and quite simply relished that role. After beating Chile and losing to Bolivia no one expected anything against mighty Argentina, twice world champions in the last 17 years. But the U.S. played with confidence and power and won one of the greatest victories of the U.S. soccer team up to that time.

The U.S. then had the pleasure of beating Mexico on penalties in the quarterfinals. In the semifinals, world champions Brazil proved too strong for the rough-and-tumble Americans but Brazil only won by a single goal. The U.S. then lost against Colombia in a match for third place.

This result was one of the signs that the U.S. soccer team was becoming much stronger than it had ever been.

Copa América
Uruguay

Date	Opponent	Result		U.S. Goals
7-8-95	Chile	2–1	○	Wynalda 2
7-11-95	Bolivia	0–1	○	
7-14-95	Argentina	3–0	○	Klopas, Lalas, Wynalda
7-17-95	Mexico	0–0*(4–1)*	○	
7-20-95	Brazil	0–1	○	
7-22-95	Colombia	1–4	○	Moore (p)

* After extra time and penalties.

DEFEATING SPAIN

As winners of the previous Gold Cup the USA took part in the 2009 Confederations Cup with other continental champions. The team didn't exactly shine at the beginning and after two games seemed to heading straight home. A comfortable win over Egypt, the African champions, in the last round of the group stage, together with good results (for the U.S.) in other games meant that the team did have to play a semifinal game against the almost unbeatable European champions.

The Spanish team sheet read like a litany of superstars: Iker Casillas, Sergio Ramos, Carles Puyol, Xabi Alonso, Cece Fabregas, Xavi, David Villa, Fernando Torres . . .

As expected Spain dominated, but the U.S. put up a strong fight and managed to keep away every ball that the Spanish threw (or rather kicked) at them, while scoring two goals of their own.

The U.S. then met Brazil again in the final and incredibly, seemed headed for another upset, leading 2–0 at the half with after a powerful performance— the goals scored, almost inevitably, by Dempsey and Donovan. In the second half, however, Brazil once again demonstrated its true skill and finally defeated the combative Americans.

Cesc Fabregas of Spain is tackled by U.S. midfielder Michael Bradley. He was born in 1987 in New Jersey and joined the highly successful team AS Roma Italy in 2012.

The 2009 Confederations Cup
South Africa

Date	Opponent	Result	U.S. Goals
6-15-09	Italy	1–3 ○	Donovan (p)
6-18-09	Brazil	0–3 ○	
6-21-09	Egypt	3–0 ○	Davies, Bradley, Dempsey
6-24-09	Spain	2–0 ○	Altidore, Dempsey
6-28-09	Brazil	2–3 ○	Dempsey, Donovan

THE MIGHTY GOALKEEPERS

The U.S. has for the past two decades been blessed with four exceptional goalkeepers.

MEOLA

A native of New Jersey, Tony Meola was the first choice goalie at the World Cups in 1990 and 1994. Although Keller and Friedel then replaced him at the top of the pecking order, he continued to play regularly for the national team, finally ending his career at 37. He played for teams like the NY/NJ Metro Stars and the NY Red Bulls, but longest for the Kansas City Wizards.

KELLER

Kasey Keller was born in Olympia, Washington, and started his career with the Portland Timbers. He then left for Europe, playing with various teams in England, notably Tottenham Hotspur from 2001–05. In Spain he played with Rayo Vallecano and in Germany with Borussia Mönchengladbach. He ended his career with the Seattle Sounders.

Keller's finest hour came when the U.S. defeated world champions Brazil at the Gold Cup in 1998. Keller made 10 world class saves, prompting legendary Brazilian striker Romário to remark: "This is the best performance by a goalkeeper I have ever seen." Romário even congratulated Keller on his heroics during the game!

MEOLA
b. 1969
1989–2006
100 games

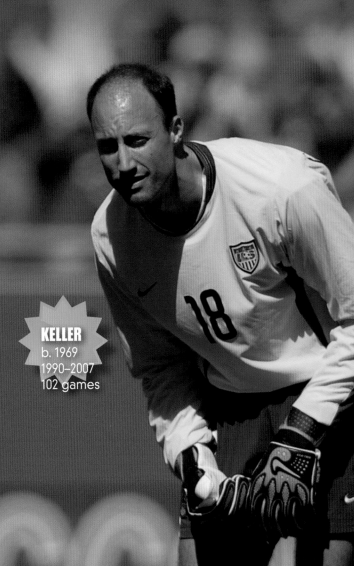

KELLER
b. 1969
1990–2007
102 games

FRIEDEL

A native of Lakewood, Ohio, Brad Friedel tried his luck with various European teams (including Turkey's Galatasaray and England's Liverpool) before settling in at Blackburn Rovers in the English Premier League. He stayed there from 2000–2008, becoming the fans' favorite, even scoring one goal from open play. Then he signed with Aston Villa and finally, at an age when most soccer players have long since retired, Friedel started playing for one of the Premier League's strongest teams, Tottenham. In spite of strong competition from other much younger goalkeepers, he still plays regularly.

Friedel played his first international game in 1992, before becoming a professional. At first in Keller's shadow, Friedel was first choice goalkeeper during the U.S.'s successful run at the 2002 World Cup, saving penalties against both Poland and South Korea. He retired from U.S. National Team duty in February of 2005.

HOWARD

Tim Howard was born in New Jersey and saw his career take off with the NY/NJ MetroStars in 1998. From 2003–2006 he played for one of the world's strongest teams, Manchester United, in England. From there he went to neighboring Everton, where he has already become a legend.

Howard played his first international against Ecuador. When Keller and Friedel retired (finally!) he became first choice keeper and has as yet no serious rival for that position. Brad Guzan of Aston Villa has established himself as Howard's back-up.

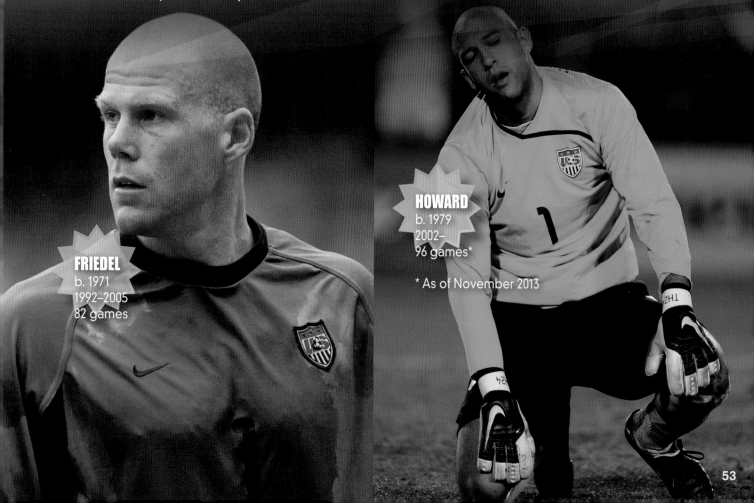

HOWARD
b. 1979
2002–
96 games*

* As of November 2013

FRIEDEL
b. 1971
1992–2005
82 games

HEADING FOR BRAZIL

In June 2012, the U.S. entered the third round of the CONCACAF qualification tournament for the 2014 World Cup. As expected, Jamaica, Guatemala, and the tiny Antigua & Barbuda proved no obstacle for Klinsmann's team, though it did lose one game.

Date	Opponent	Result	U.S. Goals
6-8-12	Antigua & Barbuda	3–1 ○	Bocanegra, Dempsey (p), Gomez
6-12-12	Guatemala	1–1 ◐	Dempsey
9-7-12	Jamaica	1–2 ○	Dempsey
9-11-12	Jamaica	1–0 ○	Gomez
10-12-12	Antigua & Barbuda	2–1 ○	E. Johnson 2
10-16-12	Guatemala	3–1 ○	Bocanegra, Dempsey 2

The Results of Group A

	Games	Won	Drawn	Lost	Goals for	Goals against	Goals differ.	Points
United States	6	4	1	1	11	6	+5	13
Jamaica	6	3	1	2	9	6	+3	10
Guatemala	6	3	1	2	9	8	+1	10
Antigua & Barbuda	6	0	1	5	4	13	-9	1

THE HEXAGONAL

The fourth and final stage of the CONCACAF qualifiers is referred to as the "Hexagonal" because of the six teams competing. The U.S. team lost their first game but won the next. The following game was a scoreless draw with Mexico in the Azteca Stadium in Mexico City. Even though coach Klinsmann fielded a team of inexperienced central defenders, the newcomers stood their guard and held the Mexican sharpshooters at bay. This was the first time since 1997 that the Americans had left the Azteca Stadium without a loss.

Klinsmann was not rid of all his worries despite the fact that his team frequently played well and triumphed during the summer of 2013, where it confidently won the Gold Cup (see page 49.) The coach had a hard time finding free-scoring forwards who would be able to break the strong defense of European and South American nations at the World Cup in Brazil. Wingers or attacking midfielders Dempsey and Donovan still seemed to be the only regular goal providers. Halfway through the Hexagonal, Jozy Altidore finally took off, while Klinsmann kept trying out different players on his side in the attack. In the end, the U.S. breezily sailed to victory in the Hexagonal. The Mexican team's awful performance was noteworthy, and for a time it seemed like this would be the first time since 1990 (when the Mexicans were disqualified) that this great CONCACAF powerhouse would not make it to the World Cup. Ironically, the success of the U.S. team during the previous World Cup competitions turned out to be Mexico's ticket for entering the World Cup. The fourth place in the Hexagonal had not, up until that time, been enough to earn a place in the World Cup finals.

However, the recent success of CONCACAF teams, especially the U.S., resulted in Mexico getting a second chance, and they managed to defeat New Zealand in an intercontinental playoff. So "the eternal rivals" both headed for Brazil.

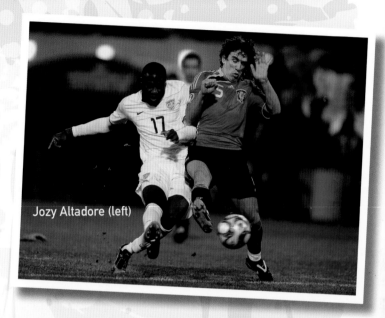

Jozy Altadore (left)

Date	Opponent	Result	U.S. Goals
2-6-13	Honduras	1–2 ○	Dempsey
3-22-13	Costa Rica	1–0 ○	Dempsey
3-26-13	Mexico	0–0 ◐	
6-7-13	Jamaica	2–1 ○	Altidore, Evans
6-11-13	Panama	2–0 ○	Altidore, E. Johnson
6-18-13	Honduras	1–0 ○	Altidore
9-6-13	Costa Rica	1–3 ○	Dempsey (p)
9-10-13	Mexico	2–0 ○	E. Johnson, Donovan
10-11-13	Jamaica	2–0 ○	Zusi, Altidore
10-15-13	Panama	3–2 ○	Orozco, Zusi, Jóhannsson

	Games	Won	Drawn	Lost	Goals for	Goals against	Goals differ.	Points
United States	10	7	1	2	15	8	+7	22
Costa Rica	10	5	3	2	13	7	+6	18
Honduras	10	4	3	3	13	12	+1	15
Mexico	10	2	5	3	7	9	-2	11
Panama	10	1	5	4	10	14	-4	8
Jamaica	10	0	5	5	5	13	-8	5

SIX FACTS

Despite the great success of several American soccer players, the United States has yet to acquire a player who can be counted among the world's very best players. Many believed that the U.S. had found this player when Freddy Adu burst onto the scene in 2004. Adu was born in Ghana but moved to Maryland when he was eight years old and his mother won the green card lottery. At the age of 14, the daring offensive midfielder became the youngest soccer player ever to score a goal in the MLS. He then played with D.C. United. At 16, Adu became the youngest player to play for the U.S. national team. By then he was attracting attention from strong European soccer clubs. Adu went to Benfica in Portugal in 2007. Sadly it turned out that Adu didn't become a soccer legend. The United States still awaits its very own Pelé, Maradona, or Messi!

Archie Stark was a relentless goal scorer with Bethlehem Steel in Pennsylvania from 1924–1930. In 221 games, Stark scored 240 goals! He was born in Scotland but moved to the U.S. at the age of 13. Stark only played two national games for his adopted country, both of which were friendly games against Canada. On August 11, 1925, Stark scored five goals in a 6–1 rout in Brooklyn. No U.S. player has scored more goals in a single game.

The U.S. team's biggest victory came in a qualifying game for the 2010 World Cup. The opponent was Barbados and the score ended 8–0. Dempsey and Brian Ching scored two goals each; one was an own goal and Donovan, Michael Bradley and Eddie Johnson scored the rest. The second biggest win in a competitive game was also against Barbados, a 7–0 thrashing in a 2002 qualifying game. Joe-Max Moore scored two goals and the other five were provided by Eddie Pope, Brian McBride, John O'Brien, Tab Ramos, and Earnie Stewart.

In consecutive friendlies in November and December 1993, the U.S. crushed the Cayman Islands 8–1 and then El Salvador 7–0. In the two games, Joe-Max Moore scored two and four goals, respectively.

The U.S. team's worst defeat was a disgraceful 11–0 against Norway in a friendly game on August 6, 1948. The second worst was the humbling 10–0 against England on May 27, 1964.

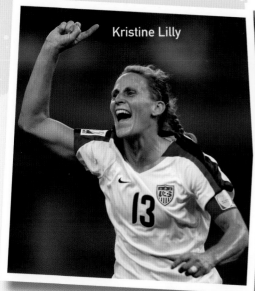

Kristine Lilly

Michelle Akers

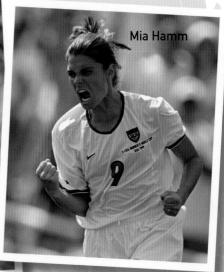

Mia Hamm

While the U.S. men's team has, as of yet, not come close to winning the World Cup, the women's team has already won the Women's World Cup twice before it was canceled. It has also won the CONCACAF Gold Cup six of the seven times it has competed.

Kristine Lilly is the most capped player in the history of soccer, both men's and women's, with her 352 games from 1987–2010.

Michelle Akers was the greatest scorer of the team in the early years, and was named FIFA Female Player of the Century in 2000, the same year she retired.

Mia Hamm held the record for international goals, more than any other player, male or female, in soccer history with her 158 goals until 2013. She also has 144 assists. Hamm played 275 games between 1987 and 2004.

Hamm's record was broken by fellow American Abby Wambach, who has scored 163 goals as of November 2013.

In 2007 English superstar David Beckham left the Spanish powerhouse Real Madrid

David Beckham

and joined the LA Galaxy. He was the most famous soccer player since Pelé, in 1975, to join an American team, which showed that the MLS was now being taken seriously by the world. After Beckham a considerable number of European and South Americans stars have followed in his footsteps, such as Thierry Henry and Robbie Keane.

THE RECORD BREAKER

THE GOALS...AND THE GAMES

The USA plays more international games than most European or South Amercian teams. Therefore U.S. players tend to amass a great number of games.

Rank	Player	Goals	Caps	Years
1	Landon Donovan	57	154	2000–
2	Clint Dempsey	36	101	2004–
3	Eric Wynalda	34	106	1990–2000
4	Brian McBride	30	95	1993–2006
5	Joe-Max Moore	24	100	1992–2002
6-7	Jozy Altidore	21	65	2007–
6-7	Bruce Murray	21	86	1985–1993
8	Eddie Johnson	19	60	2004–
9–10	Earnie Stewart	17	101	1990–2004
9–10	DaMarcus Beasley	17	113	2001–
11	Cobi Jones	15	164	1992–2004
12	Carlos Bocanegra	14	110	2001–2012
13–14	Hugo Perez	13	73	1984–1994
13–14	Marcelo Balboa	13	127	1988–2000
15–16	Frank Klopas	12	40	1988–1996
15–16	Clint Mathis	12	46	1998–2005
17–19	Brian Ching	11	45	2003–2010
17–19	Peter Vermes	11	67	1988–1997
17–19	Michael Bradley	11	81	2006–
20	Eddie Lewis	10	82	1996–2008

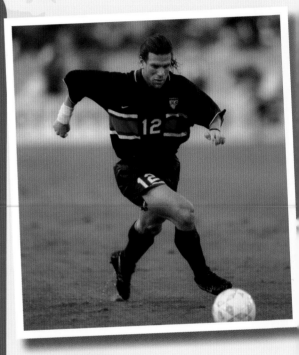

JEFF AGOOS b. 1968

When Agoos started playing for the U.S. team it was still considered a lowly soccer power, but when he retired 15 years later it was busy establishing itself among the strongest in the world. Agoos grew up in California. He played for D.C. United, San Jose Earthquakes, and NY/NJ MetroStars in the MLS. Agoos was a determined defender who surprisingly played only three games for the USA in World Cup finals. That was in 2002.

Rank	Player	Caps	Goals	Years
1	Cobi Jones	164	15	1992–2004
2	Landon Donovan	154	57	2000–
3	Jeff Agoos	134	4	1988–2003
4	Marcelo Balboa	127	13	1988–2000
5	DaMarcus Beasley	113	17	2001–
6	Claudio Reyna	112	8	1994–2006
7-8	Carlos Bocanegra	110	14	2001–2012
7-8	Paul Caligiuri	110	5	1984–1997
9	Eric Wynalda	106	34	1990–2000
10	Kasey Keller	102	0	1990–2007
11–12	Clint Dempsey	101	36	2004–
11–12	Earnie Stewart	101	17	1990–2004
13–14	Joe-Max Moore	100	24	1992–2002
13–14	Tony Meola	100	0	1988–2002
15	Alexi Lalas	96	9	1991–1998
16–17	Brian McBride	95	30	1993–2006
16–17	Tim Howard	95	0	2002–
18	John Harkes	90	6	1987–2000
19	Steve Cherundolo	87	2	1999–2012
20	Bruce Murray	86	21	1985–1993

COBI JONES b. 1970

He was born in Detroit but grew up in California. After starting his professional career with Coventry City in England he joined the LA Galaxy when the new Major League Soccer began in 1996. He played with the team for the rest of his long and illustrious career.

In 1992 he played his first game for the national team and by time he retired in 2004 he had played more games than any other male American in history. Jones was a powerful central midfielder, always ready to fight to the last moment.

DaMARCUS BEASLEY

b. 1982. One of the most versatile players of the U.S. team, Beasley was born in Indiana in 1982. He has played for the Glasgow Rangers in Scotland, Manchester City in England, and Puebla in Mexico, among other teams. He usually plays as a left winger but can and has played both as a striker and a center back.

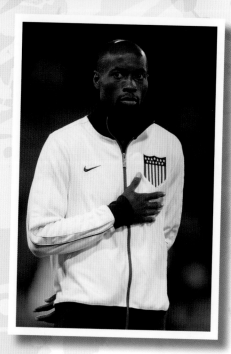

DEMPSEY

Born in Nacogdoches, Texas, Clint Dempsey began his professional career with the New England Revolution. In 2007, he joined fellow U.S. international players Carlos Bocanegra and Brian McBride at Fulham in the English Premier League. He played there for five years with great success, and was voted Fulham Player of the Season by fans for two consecutive seasons. In 2012, he went to EPL powerhouse Tottenham and became the highest paid U.S. soccer player of all time, but a year later he then transferred to the Seattle Sounders.

Dempsey played his first international game in 2004 and has since become one of the U.S. team's most dangerous attacking players. In 2009, he was voted Man of the Match when the U.S. defeated Spain in the famous Confederation Cup game (see page 51.)

DEMPSEY
b. 1983
2004–
101 games*
36 goals*

* As of November 2013

He has been selected U.S. Soccer Athlete of the Year three times and the Honda Player of the Year twice.

Dempsey is an extremely aggressive attacking player, who can play any role in the offensive line. He has often played as a striker, second striker, or attacking midfielder but has recently been employed mainly as a winger.

THE USA COUNTS ON THESE TWO!

DONOVAN

Landon Donovan was born in Ontario, California, and began his professional career with Bayer Leverkusen in the German Bundesliga. Donovan then returned to the States and played so successfully for the San Jose Earthquakes that he was named U.S. Soccer Athlete of the year in 2003, at only 21 years old. A year later, he was again named for the honor, and then also in 2009 and 2010, becoming the first and only player ever to receive this award four times.

Since 2002, the national sports media has chosen Donovan no less than seven times as their Honda Player of the Year.

From 2005, Donovan has played for the LA Galaxy with great results, scoring and assisting almost at will. He formed a strong relationship with David Beckham on the field from 2007–2012. He was also on loan to Bayern Munich and Everton at various times.

Donovan burst onto the international scene during the 2002 World Cup where he was named Best Young Player of the competition. He has since played a leading role in every competition the U.S. has taken part in, and has already broken all scoring and assisting records.

Donovan can play any attacking role for his team, but is most at home playing as a very aggressive winger, sometimes functioning as a second (or even third) striker.

Learn more!

Websites

- Wikipedia has a great site on the the U.S. team, the players, the coaches, and practically everything else!
- The American Soccer History Archives: http://homepages.sover. net/~spectrum/index.html, a fabulous site with information about every aspect of the U.S. team from 1909. Also a very good bibliography and list of recources on the web. Highly recommended.
- http://www.ussoccer.com/, the homepage of the U.S. Soccer Federation. A wealth of information about both current activities and history. See especially the section on the U.S. Soccer Hall of Fame: http://www.ussoccer.com/about/history/hall-of-fame.aspx

Glossary

Striker: A forward player positioned closest to the opposing goal who has the primary role of receiving the ball from teammates and delivering it to the goal.

Winger: The player who keeps to the margins of the field and receives the ball from midfielders or defenders and then sends it forward to the awaiting strikers.

Offensive midfielder: This player is positioned behind the team's forwards and seeks to take the ball through the opposing defense. They either pass to the strikers or attempt a goal themselves. This position is sometimes called "number 10" in reference to the Brazilian genius Pelé, who more or less created this role and wore shirt number 10.

Defensive midfielder: Usually plays in front of his team's defense. The player's central role is to break the offense of the opposing team and deliver the ball to their team's forwards. The contribution of these players is not always obvious but they nevertheless play an important part in the game.

Central midfielder: The role of the central midfielder is divided between offense and defense. The player mainly seeks to secure the center of the field for their team. Box-to-box midfielders are versatile players who possess such strength and foresight that they constantly spring between the penalty areas.

Fullbacks (either left back or right back): Players who defend the sides of the field, near their own goal, but also dash up the field overlapping with wingers in order to lob the ball into the opponent's goal. The fullbacks are sometimes titled wing backs if they are expected to play a bigger role in the offense.

Center backs: These players are the primary defenders of their teams, and are two or three in number depending on formation. The purpose of the center backs is first and foremost to prevent the opponents from scoring and then send the ball towards the center.

Sweeper: The original purpose of the sweeper was to stay behind the defending teammates and "sweep up" the ball if they happened to lose it, but also to take the ball forward. The position of the sweeper has now been replaced by defensive midfielders.

Goalkeeper: Prevents the opponent's goals and is the only player who is allowed to use their hands!